Easy to Intermediate Piano Solo

THE WORLD'S GREAT CLASSICAL MUSIC

The Romantic Era

102 Selections from Symphonies, Ballets, Operas & Piano Literature
for Piano Solo

EDITED BY BLAKE NEELY AND RICHARD WALTERS

Cover Painting: John Constable, *The Hay-Wain*, 1821

ISBN: 978-0-634-04809-8

Visit Hal Leonard Online at
www.halleonard.com

Contact us:
Hal Leonard
7777 West Bluemound Road
Milwaukee, WI 53213
Email: info@halleonard.com

In Europe, contact:
Hal Leonard Europe Limited
42 Wigmore Street
Marylebone, London, W1U 2RN
Email: info@halleonardeurope.com

In Australia, contact:
Hal Leonard Australia Pty. Ltd.
4 Lentara Court
Cheltenham, Victoria, 3192 Australia
Email: info@halleonard.com.au

CONTENTS

Alexander Borodin	14	Polovetzian Dance (from the opera *Prince Igor*), First Theme
Johannes Brahms	9	Lullaby (Wiegenlied)
	10	Symphony No. 1 in C Minor, Op. 68, Fourth Movement Excerpt
	12	Symphony No. 4 in E Minor, Op. 98, First Movement Excerpt
Anton Bruckner	17	Symphony No. 7, Second Movement Excerpt
Fryderyk Chopin	23	Mazurka in E Minor, Op. 17, No. 2*
	31	Mazurka in F Major, Op. 68, No. 3 (Posthumous)*
	20	Mazurka in G Minor, Op. 67, No. 2 (Posthumous)*
	26	Nocturne in C-sharp Minor, Op. Posthumous*
	35	Polonaise in G Minor, Op. Posthumous*
	30	Prelude in A Major, Op. 28, No. 7*
	38	Prelude in B Minor, Op. 28, No. 6*
	34	Prelude in C Minor, Op. 28, No. 20*
	40	Prelude in E Minor, Op. 28, No. 4*
	42	Waltz in B Minor, Op. 69, No. 2 (Posthumous)*
	48	Waltz in F Minor, Op. 70, No. 2*
César Franck	51	Panis angelicus
Charles Gounod	54	Funeral March of a Marionette, Themes
Edvard Grieg	76	In the Hall of the Mountain King (from *Peer Gynt*)
		Selections from *Lyric Pieces, Book 1*, Op. 12:*
	56	Arietta
	58	Album Leaf
	61	Elves' Dance
	67	Waltz
	64	Watchman's Song
		Selections from *Lyric Pieces, Book 9*, Op. 68:*
	70	Cradle Song
	72	Grandmother's Minuet
Cornelius Gurlitt		Selections from *Album Leaves for the Young*, Op. 101:*
	81	The Fair
	84	March
	86	Slumber Song
Stephen Heller	91	Avalanche, Op. 45, No. 2*
	88	The Brook, Op 45, No.1*
	94	Etude in C Major, Op. 47, No. 19*
	98	Prelude in C Minor, Op. 119, No. 25*
	100	Song of May, Op. 45, No. 5*
	97	The Tolling Bell, Op. 125, No. 8*
Edward MacDowell	104	To a Wild Rose (from *Woodland Sketches*), Op. 51*
Gustav Mahler	106	Symphony No. 5, Fourth Movement Excerpt (Adagietto)
Jules Massenet	136	Meditation (from the opera *Thaïs*)
Felix Mendelssohn		Selections from *Songs Without Words*, Op. 19:*
	110	Confidence
	112	Regrets
	116	Venetian Boat Song No. 1
		Selections from *Songs Without Words*, Op. 30:*
	118	Consolation
	122	Venetian Boat Song No. 2
		Selections from *Songs Without Words*, Op. 102:*
	120	Faith
	125	Tarantella

Pieces originally for piano solo; the remaining works are piano transcriptions.

	128	"Fingal's Cave" Overture (The Hebrides), Themes
	130	Gondola Song in A Major (1837)*
	133	Symphony No. 4 ("Italian"), Op. 90, First Movement Excerpt

Sergei Rachmaninoff 139 Piano Concerto No. 2, First Movement Excerpt

Nikolay Rimsky-Korsakov 146 *Sheherazade*, Themes from Part 1

Franz Schubert 153 Andante in C Major (1812)*
152 Ecossaise in D Major, Op. 33, No. 2*
158 Moment Musicale, Op. 94, No. 3*
156 Symphony No. 9 ("The Great"), D 944, First Movement Excerpt
162 Waltz in A Major, Op. 50, No. 13*
164 Waltz in A Minor, Op. 77, No. 9*
161 Waltz in A-flat Major, Op. 9, No. 12*
166 Waltz in A-flat Major, Op. 33, No. 15*
168 Waltz in B Minor, Op. 18a, No. 5*
167 Waltz in F Minor, Op. 33, No. 14*
170 Waltz in G Major, Op. 67, No. 15*

Robert Schumann Selections from *Kinderszenen* (Scenes from Childhood), Op. 15:*
172 A Child Falling Asleep
174 Curious Story
176 Frightening
178 An Important Event
182 Perfectly Contented
181 Pleading Child
180 The Poet Speaks
171 Of Strange Lands and People
184 Träumerei

Selections from *Album für die Jugend* (Album for the Young), Op. 68:*
186 First Loss
187 The Happy Farmer Returning from Work
188 Hunting Song
189 Melody
190 The Reaper's Song
192 Soldier's March
193 The Wild Horseman

194 Bagatelle*
196 Cradle Song (from *Album Leaves*, Op. 124)*
198 Evensong (from Sonata in D Major, Op. 118b)*
200 Fantasy Dance, Op. 124, No. 5*
202 Waltz, Op. 129, No. 4*

Johann Strauss, Jr. 207 By the Beautiful Blue Danube, Themes
204 Tales from the Vienna Woods, Themes

Pyotr Il'yich Tchaikovsky 212 1812 Overture, Excerpt

Selections from *Album for Children* (Album pour enfants), Op. 39:*
220 In Church
222 The Hobby Horse
226 Italian Song
228 Mazurka
225 Morning Prayer
230 Old French Song
231 The Organ Grinder
232 Polka
234 Russian Song
235 The Sick Doll
236 The Song of the Lark
238 Sweet Dream
241 Waltz in E-flat Major

217 Dance of the Sugar Plum Fairy (from the ballet *The Nutcracker*)
244 Piano Concerto No. 1, First Movement Excerpt
248 Romeo and Juliet Fantasy Overture, "Love Theme"
252 Waltz of the Flowers (from the ballet *The Nutcracker*), Excerpt

ABOUT THE COMPOSERS...

ALEXANDER BORODIN (1833-1887).

Alexander Borodin's success as a composer is astounding in the light of his double life. Borodin was a member of the Moguchaya Kuchka (Mighty Handful, or Mighty Five), a group of the five great Russian nationalist composers that included Balakirev, Borodin, Cui, Musorgsky and Rimsky-Korsakov. His works were known internationally during his lifetime and the "Polovetsian Dances," from his opera *Prince Igor*, remains a favorite in the classical repertoire today. The other side of Borodin's double life was an enormously successful career in medicine. As a child the composer taught himself the cello while pursuing a fascination with science. As an adult, his musical interests were always secondary to his research and lecturing. He taught at the Medico-Surgical Academy in St. Petersburg, traveling throughout Europe to give papers and lectures. Borodin allied himself with the Russian nationalists, making use of Russian folk songs and folk melodies in his works. He first achieved international recognition as a composer with *On the Steppes of Central Asia*. In addition to three symphonies, chamber music and vocal pieces, Borodin wrote five operas during his lifetime. Of the five, he completed only one, *Bogatïri* (The Bogatïrs). His greatest work was the opera *Prince Igor*, on which he worked from 1869 through 1887. Unfinished at the time of his death, the work was completed and partially orchestrated by Glazunov and Rimsky-Korsakov. Although it is based on Borodin's own libretto, which has been called weak and disjointed, the opera contains a great deal of remarkable music.

JOHANNES BRAHMS (1833-1897).

Johannes Brahms was a man of strong opinions. He disapproved of the "New German School" of composers, namely Liszt and Wagner. He avoided what he believed to be the excesses of the tone poem, relying instead on traditional symphonic forms. After his Symphony No. 1 was premiered, he was hailed as "Beethoven's true heir." The symphony, written when Brahms was forty-three years old, is so clearly linked to the symphonies of Beethoven that it is jokingly been called "Beethoven's Tenth." Brahms began his musical studies as a youngster, gaining experience in composition and working as an arranger for his father's light orchestra. He revered composer Robert Schumann. On the advice of Franz Liszt he met Schumann, with whom he developed a close friendship. He also developed a deep love for Schumann's wife, Clara Wieck Schumann. From the time of Schumann's mental breakdown until his death in 1856, Brahms and Clara tended to the ailing composer. The truth of the relationship between Brahms and Clara Schumann remains something of a mystery. Brahms never married. Clara Schumann never re-married following Robert's death. When Clara Schumann died in May of 1896, Brahms did not get to the funeral due to a missed train connection. He died the following April. Throughout his life, Brahms would sign letters "Frei aber froh" (Free but happy), until his last years when he signed "Frei aber einsam," (Free but lonely). One of the pall-bearers at Brahms' funeral was the composer Antonín Dvořák.

ANTON BRUCKNER (1824-1896).

Austrian composer and organist Anton Bruckner was one of the more controversial figures of the Romantic era. An unwitting musical revolutionary, he came of age as a composer in an era during which the concert-going public was deeply divided between the music of Brahms and the music of Wagner. He and his music were caught up in the public war between followers of the two great composers. Much of his music was not fully appreciated by international audiences until years after his death. Bruckner was a deeply religious man from humble beginnings. He was middle-aged by the time he arrived in Vienna, sporting country manners, dress and accent, and possessing virtually no social sophistication. He retained his dress and customs, and never grew comfortable in Viennese society. Part of Bruckner's social naiveté stemmed from his many years in a monastery. He was enrolled as a monastery chorister at 13, following his father's death, and later taught at the same monastery for ten years. He left the monastery at 31, when he won the post of cathedral organist in the city of Linz. In the ten years he spent in Linz, Bruckner was exposed to the music of Wagner, which broke many of the rules of composition that he had been taught, but achieved a musical level to which he aspired. Although he became a revolutionary in his own way, he never saw himself in this light. He broke musical ground by taking Wagner's use of descriptive themes and harmonic freedom to new levels. When he was 44 he accepted a professorship at the Vienna Conservatory, where he would spend the rest of his life. Throughout his life, Bruckner was plagued by bouts of depression, shyness and a very poor opinion of himself. The harsh criticism lobbed at him from the Brahmsians hurt him deeply.

FRYDERYK CHOPIN (1810-1849).

Although composer and pianist Fryderyk Chopin was born to a French father and spent half of his life in Paris, he always defined himself by the land of his birth, Poland. Throughout his life he retained strong nationalistic feelings. Chopin the pianist achieved the status of an idol. His mystique was based in part on his cultured upbringing and in part on his fragile good looks. His sensitive nature, frail health, and self-imposed exile only intensified the public's fascination with him. In 1831, after receiving his training and achieving some success in Poland, Chopin moved to Paris. There he found himself one of many piano virtuosos. Although he quickly made a name for himself, his temperament and physical frailty, caused by tuberculosis that plagued him throughout much of his life, left him poorly suited to life as a performer. He gave only about 30 performances, many of which were private affairs. From 1838 to 1847 Chopin was romantically involved with novelist Georges Sand (Aurore Dudevant). The years of their stormy romance were his most productive as a composer. While Franz Liszt created works of grand proportions and brilliant virtuosity, Chopin remained a miniaturist, creating elegant, fluid melodies within the framework of small pieces. He was the only great composer who wrote almost exclusively for the piano. Chopin is set apart from other Romantic era composers by the fact that his works were not inspired by or based upon literature, works of art, or political ideals. Composition was difficult work for Chopin, who was a gifted improviser from his earliest days. He composed as he played, finding it painful to commit his work to paper. When Chopin and Georges Sand parted ways in 1847, the composer's frail health took a turn for the worse. He was further weakened by his 1848 concert tour of England. When he died in October of 1849, public fascination only increased, as evidenced by the nearly 3,000 mourners who attended his funeral.

CÉSAR FRANCK (1822-1890).

Belgian-born César Franck was largely overlooked during his lifetime, at least as a composer. After receiving his education in France, and spending his career there as well, he was awarded the ribbon of the Chevalier of the Legion of Honor from the French government for his work as a professor of organ. There was no mention of his compositions. Franck's father was a banker who, unlike the fathers of most aspiring musicians, actually wanted a career in music for his son. He was delighted when, at age eleven, his son began touring as a virtuoso pianist. He was far less delighted when it became apparent that his son was bound for obscurity as a church organist and composer. Although he was respected as a performer and teacher throughout his life, he had to wait until he was sixty-eight for his first real success as a composer. It was the premiere of his String Quartet in D Major that brought him this public acclaim. In 1879 he was publicly snubbed when only two of the guests he invited to hear the premiere of his oratorio actually attended. Franck was deeply religious and took great pleasure in his service to the church as an organist. The premiere of his Symphony in D Minor, one of his enduring works, was a failure. The orchestra objected to his including the English horn in a symphony and looked disdainfully on a piece by an organ professor. Franck sought to write Romantic music within a Classical framework. He loved to juxtapose diverse sounding instruments. "Panis angelicus" a sacred piece, was composed in the early eighteen-seventies for tenor, organ, harp, cello and double bass.

CHARLES GOUNOD (1818-1893).

While French composer Charles Gounod was in Rome competing for the Prix de Rome, which he won on his third try in 1839, he discovered sixteenth-century polyphonic music wafting about the Sistine Chapel. He was so moved by this music, and likely by the setting as well, that he considered becoming a priest. Instead, he began composing masses and worked as a church organist in Paris. When he began writing operas, he leaned heavily on the examples of Gluck and Meyerbeer. Although these first operas were failures, he soon found his own voice, creating the likes of *Roméo et Juliette* and *Faust*. With *Faust* he struck a blow for French composers. *Faust*, although not a resounding success at the outset, was a powerful opera that came from the pen of a Frenchman. The opera put a dent in the domination of foreign operas in Paris and opened doors for other aspiring French composers. In the fifty years that followed, *Faust* was performed some two thousand times in Paris alone. It was the opera that opened the new Metropolitan Opera Company in New York in 1883. Gounod weathered the Franco-Prussian war living in England, becoming the first conductor of the Royal Albert Hall Choral Society. He returned to Paris in 1875, where he continued to work on operas. From 1881 to the end of his life he wrote almost exclusively church music. Like Mozart, he began a requiem that would prove to be his own. He was sitting at the piano, working on the Requiem, when he slumped onto the keyboard. He died three days later. Gounod's "Funeral March of a Marionette," written in 1873, is best known to television audiences as the Alfred Hitchcock theme.

EDVARD GRIEG (1843-1907).

Edvard Grieg holds a unique position in music history as not just the most famous of Norwegian composers, but as one of the only Norwegian composers to have achieved an international reputation. Grieg drew upon traditional Norwegian folk songs for the inspiration and basis for many of his pieces. His incorporation of national folk music into classical forms inspired musicians throughout Europe to do the same with the traditional music of their own countries. Although Grieg's Piano Concerto in A Minor is his best known work, it is not typical of his style. Most of his pieces are small in scale, giving him a reputation as a miniaturist. Grieg's first music lessons came from his mother. When Norwegian violinist Ole Bull heard the teen-aged Grieg play the piano, he arranged for him to enter the Leipzig Conservatory in Germany. Although the young musician was terribly homesick, living so far from home, he enjoyed the opportunity to hear performances by such luminaries as Clara Schumann and Richard Wagner. After his studies in Germany, and later in Denmark, Grieg returned to Norway. Finding himself in demand throughout Europe, Grieg spent much of his career traveling. The recipient of honorary degrees from Cambridge and Oxford, Grieg was also honored as one of his country's foremost composers.

CORNELIUS GURLITT (1820-1901).

German pianist, organist and composer Cornelius Gurlitt was born in Altona, Germany, near Hamburg. Although he spent a portion of his career in the city of his birth, he traveled and worked throughout Europe for many years. Gurlitt made his first public performance at age seventeen and studied with J.P. Rudolf Reinecke, father of composer Carl Reinecke, as well as with Paul Weyse. He lived in Leipzig, Copenhagen, and Rome for a time, and worked as a military band leader for a bit as well. In 1851 he returned to Altona, where he became the organist at the city's main church and began teaching in Hamburg. Cornelius wrote an enormous number of piano pieces, many designed as studies for students. Although he wrote symphonies, operettas and a four-act opera, Gurlitt is best remembered today for his smaller piano pieces and studies. His brother, Louis, was a respected artist, known for his realistic paintings of landscapes. The composer's grand nephew, Willibald Gurlitt, was a renowned German musicologist. Gurlitt died in Altona at age eighty-one.

STEPHEN HELLER (1813-1888).

Born in Pest, Hungary, composer and pianist Stephen Heller studied in Vienna with Carl Czerny. He made his highly successful debut in 1828. Following that performance his father arranged an extensive tour for the young performer. Lasting nearly two years, the tour led to Heller's collapse from nervous exhaustion in Augsburg. Although he intended to stay just a few weeks in Augsburg to recover from the collapse, he remained there for eight years. While in Augsburg, he received praise from pianist and critic Robert Schumann, in Schumann's *Neue Zeitschrift für Musik*, and eventually wrote as a critic for that publication under the pseudonym "Jeanquirit." Heller eventually made his way to Paris, where he was known more as a composer and teacher than as a performer. He lost his eyesight in his later years, which prompted poet Robert Browning to assist in setting up a fund to support the composer. Although Heller published more than 160 piano pieces, some of his other compositions were never published, including a set of Lieder based on writings of Goethe that are believed to reside in a private collection in Augsburg. His works include character pieces, operatic transcriptions, fantasies, sonatas, nocturnes, waltzes, caprices, and scherzos. However, it is his short studies that drew the most attention and are best remembered today.

EDWARD MACDOWELL (1860-1908).

Edward MacDowell was the first American musician to achieve an international reputation. Born in New York, the pianist and composer studied in Paris, Wiesbaden and Frankfurt, and eventually took a teaching post at the Darmstadt Conservatory. Pianist Franz Liszt was a supporter of MacDowell's music and heard the young man play several times. In 1888 MacDowell returned to the United States, settling in Boston. Financial pressures led him to focus his time and attention on performances rather than on his compositions for a time, but he eventually found a comfortable balance in his professional life, winning recognition as a performer, teacher and composer. In 1896 he was offered a post as Professor of Music at Columbia University in New York. His post was the first of its kind at Columbia, which was in the process of creating a music department at the time. In New York, MacDowell wrote some of his most enduring piano music. By the end of 1904 he was suffering from obvious signs of the mental illness which caused his death four years later at age forty-seven. During his last years he had the idea of turning his summer home in Peterborough, Vermont into a colony for artists. The MacDowell Colony is still in operation today and has housed many notable American composers such as Aaron Copland, Virgil Thomson and Leonard Bernstein.

GUSTAV MAHLER (1860-1911).

Gustav Mahler was not exactly a musician's musician. His perfectionism caused him to alienate many of the musicians with whom he worked. When he became music director of the Vienna Royal Opera he cleaned house, replacing orchestral singers and orchestral musicians. He restaged existing productions, seeing to every detail of the productions himself. The musicians considered him heavy-handed, while the opera's management felt he was spending money wildly. Mahler was a workaholic. He devoted his summers to composition since his conducting schedule during the concert season was non-stop. As a composer he devoted his energy entirely to songs, song cycles and symphonies. The symphonies are enormous, involved, Romantic works. They were brutally treated by the critics of his day. His symphonies did not find receptive audiences until after World War II, when they found unprecedented success. Mahler left the Vienna Royal Opera, sailing for New York to conduct at the Metropolitan Opera. While in New York he became instrumental in the revitalization of the New York Philharmonic. But his inability to slow down was taking its toll. Mahler had been warned that his heart was weak and was told to cut back on his working hours. Cutting back was impossible. He worked at his usual feverish pace until he collapsed in New York on February 21, 1911. Unable to return to work, he was moved to Paris for treatments. When it became apparent that he would not recover, he asked to be moved to Vienna where he died on May 18, 1911. The story has been told that in his last hours he conducted an imaginary orchestra with a single finger. It has also been said that his last word was "Mozart."

JULES MASSENET (1842-1912).

On the way to becoming one of the most popular French composers of the latter nineteenth century, Massenet taught himself the art of orchestration by playing percussion at the Paris Opera. He struck financial success composing a series of operas based on subject matter that mixed romance and religion, culminating in his 1894 opera, *Thaïs*. His most famous operas, *Manon*, in 1884, and *Werther*, in 1892, put him at the helm of French opera for the next twenty years. A young American soprano, Sibyl Sanderson, greatly admired by the composer, premiered the role of Manon and later sang the role of Thaïs. Massenet continued to write twenty more operas, outpacing his rivals in the genre. Massenet followed the footsteps of Charles Gounod using a similarly sentimental melodic style that won him the nickname 'daughter of Gounod.' He consciously restricted his style to the tastes of the affluent Parisians, a quality that disgusted some of his envious contemporaries, like Debussy, who sought more intellect and less suavity and charm in their musical sound. However, as an unselfish, life-long teacher at the Paris Conservatory, Massenet made a lasting influence on new French composers, thus laying the foundation for stylistic departures. Massenet continued to write operas into the early twentieth century with works like *Le jongleur de Notre-Dame*, 1902, a medieval Christmas tale. It was about this same time that Debussy began to emerge and surpass Massenet as the most important French opera composer.

FELIX MENDELSSOHN (1809-1847).

While most of Mendelssohn's colleagues could tell stories of their battles with family over choice of career and even more tales of their financial struggles as musicians, Felix Mendelssohn could only listen. He was born into a wealthy family that supported his goals in music from the very first. Even in their conversion from Judaism to Christianity, which the family had long considered, they were spurred to action by thoughts of their son's future. It was at the time of their conversion that they changed the family surname to Mendelssohn-Bartholdy. Mendelssohn set out on his musical career with two clear goals. He wanted to re-introduce the largely forgotten music of old masters such as Bach to the public, and he dreamed of opening a first-rate conservatory. At the age of twenty he conducted a pioneering performance of Bach's *St. Matthew Passion*, the first of many such concerts he would lead. A few years later he founded and directed the Leipzig Conservatory. As a composer, Mendelssohn combined the expressive ideals of the Romantics with the traditional forms of the Classical era. He is remembered both as one of the great Romantic composers and one of the last of classicists. In his career Mendelssohn found success at an early age, and remained highly successful until his death. His sister Fanny, to whom he was exceptionally close, died suddenly on May 14, 1847. Shortly after he got the news of his sister's death, Mendelssohn fell unconscious, having burst a blood vessel in his head. Although he recovered from this incident, he was terribly diminished by the illness. His health and mental state deteriorated until his death on November 4 that same year. Memorial services for the great conductor/composer were held in most German cities, as well as in various cities in Great Britain, where he had become quite a celebrity.

SERGEI RACHMANINOFF (1873-1943).

Once described by composer Igor Stravinsky as "a six-and-a-half-foot-tall scowl," Sergei Rachmaninoff's stern visage was a trademark of sorts. Rachmaninoff first found fame as a pianist, touring throughout his native Russia to critical acclaim. His compositions won notice in those early years as well, including a Moscow Conservatory Gold Medal in composition. Yet the 1897 premiere of his Symphony No. 1 was a complete failure, due in large part to poor conducting by Alexander Glazunov. The dismal reception of the piece sent Rachmaninoff into a three-year creative slump that he overcame through hypnosis. During those three years he began conducting, earning international respect for his work on the podium. When his Symphony No. 1 received its London premiere in 1909, it was a huge success. Rachmaninoff made his first U.S. tour in 1909. On the tour he featured his Piano Concerto No. 3, which he had written expressly for his American audiences. Rachmaninoff fled Russia in the wake of the October Revolution of 1917. He brought his family to America where he continued to concertize, but did not compose for nearly a decade. After years of touring, Rachmaninoff decided that the 1942-43 concert season would have to be his last. In January of 1943 he began to suffer from an illness diagnosed as pleurisy. He gave what was to be his final performance on February 17. He then returned to his Beverly Hills home where he died of cancer on March 28.

NIKOLAY RIMSKY-KORSAKOV (1844-1908).

Trained as an officer in the Russian Navy, composer Rimsky-Korsakov had a great interest in music but little training beyond piano lessons. Although he displayed prodigious talents as a child, his aristocratic standing meant that a career in music was out of the question. Yet, after teaching himself counterpoint and harmony, and establishing himself as a composer, he became a professor at the St. Petersburg Conservatory. He was removed from that position when he publicly condemned the police control over the school and its students. Among his students were Alexander Glazunov and Igor Stravinsky. He is remembered as the central figure of "The Russian Five" (or "The Mighty Five"), a group of composers that included Modest Musorgsky, Alexander Borodin, César Cui and Mily Balakirev. The group favored a dynamic national style in distinct contrast to the elegant sounds of Tchaikovsky. Rimsky-Korsakov composed more than fifteen operas, numerous choral works and orchestral pieces, a great quantity of vocal music, as well as chamber works and piano pieces. Of this great quantity of music only three orchestral pieces have remained in the classical repertoire: the symphonic suite *Sheherazade* for which he is best remembered, his *Spanish Capriccio* and his *Russian Easter Festival*. Written in 1888, *Sheherazade* is based on vignettes from "Tales of the Arabian Nights."

FRANZ SCHUBERT (1797-1828).

The story of Schubert's life reads like a heartbreaking novel. Now hailed as one of the great Romantic composers, not one of Schubert's symphonies was performed during his lifetime. It was five decades after his death before any of them were published. Schubert, the son of a school headmaster, was not a virtuoso musician. Although his musical abilities were readily apparent to his teachers, his inability to perform left him with little means to support himself. He taught in his father's school for a time, but was miserable in that job. Schubert studied with Salieri, who was astounded by the young composer's abilities. After writing his first symphony at age fifteen, Schubert presented Salieri with a completed, fully orchestrated opera two years later. Schubert lived less than thirty-two years, yet he composed a phenomenal amount of music, including some six hundred songs. One hundred and forty-four of those songs date from the year 1815, a year in which he was teaching at his father's school. After Schubert left his father's school, he had the good fortune to collect a small group of devoted friends and supporters. The friends would periodically organize evenings of the composer's music, which came to be known as "Schubertiades." Schubert's health began to fail as early as 1822. When he died, at age thirty-one, he was viewed as a composer of songs. It was not the enormous number of songs that earned him this mistaken designation so much as the fact that almost none of his other music had been performed during his lifetime. In addition to the songs, Schubert completed seven symphonies, and left one unfinished. He wrote a number of operas, although these are far from his best works. He also wrote choral works, chamber music and piano pieces. In accordance with his dying wish, he was buried beside Beethoven, whom he had idolized and at whose funeral he served as a torch-bearer.

ROBERT SCHUMANN (1810-1856).

Robert Schumann's dream was to become a pianist. As the son of a German bookseller and writer, he grew up surrounded by literature and instilled with a love of music. His world crumbled however, when he was just sixteen, with the death of his father and the subsequent suicide of his sister. Schumann entered law school, but spent most of his time studying music. In 1830 he moved into the household of his piano teacher, Friedrich Wieck. Soon afterwards, his left hand began to trouble him. His career dreams were shattered when his left hand became permanently crippled. He turned his energies to composition, making a name as a music critic as well. An inspired critic, he founded the music journal *Neue Zeitschrift für Musik*, in 1834. He often wrote under the pseudonyms "Florestan" and "Eusebius." Schumann fell in love with with his teacher's daughter, Clara Wieck, a highly acclaimed concert pianist. Clara's father fought vigorously against the romance. Schumann married Clara in 1840, but only after he had taken his case to the courts. In the year he was married, the composer wrote some 150 songs, turning to orchestral music the following year. Schumann suffered from bouts of terrible depression, which became progressively worse with time. In 1854 he attempted suicide. Unable to function any longer, he was then placed in an asylum, where he spent the last two years of his life. His wife and his friend, the young composer Johannes Brahms, looked after him in those final years.

JOHANN STRAUSS, JR. (1825-1899).

Just as John Philip Sousa was America's March King, Johann Strauss Jr. was Austria's Waltz King. The Strauss family is synonymous with the waltz. Johann, Sr. was a violinist, conductor and composer, who was widely popular throughout Europe. He conducted in a flamboyant style, with violin in hand. He popularized the open-air concert and programmed many of his numerous works. His son Josef was also a conductor, working with the family orchestra and composing a number of pieces as well. Eduard, a younger son, became Vienna's imperial-royal music director from 1872-1901. He was the most respected conductor of the Strauss clan, and was in great demand throughout Europe. But it was Johann, Jr. who won the hearts of the Austrian people. His talent was recognized early and his first composition was published when he was only six years old. As an adult, he formed a rival orchestra to his father's and began to tour with his own music. Eventually the two groups were merged into a single family orchestra. While the public loved Johann, Jr., the world of classical music saw him as lacking substance. For all the criticism he received during his lifetime, his music is familiar to classical audiences a century after his death. During Johann, Jr.'s last days, the city of Vienna waited anxiously for hopeful news of his health. On June 3, 1899, a large crowd gathered for an outdoor concert. In mid performance, a messenger bolted onto the stage and whispered something into the conductor's ear. The conductor abruptly stopped the orchestra. After a few moments they began playing the opening notes of "By the Beautiful Blue Danube," Strauss' beloved waltz. The audience knew in an instant what it meant. Their Strauss had died. Rising to their feet, the men removed their hats and bowed their heads while women cried. A few days later, Johann Strauss, Jr.'s obituary referred to him as "the last symbol of cheerful, pleasant times."

PYOTR IL'YICH TCHAIKOVSKY (1840-1893).

It is a curious twist of fate that the composer of so bombastic a work as the *1812 Overture* should have been an extremely fragile individual. Exceptionally sensitive from childhood, Tchaikovsky eventually deteriorated into a precarious emotional state. Tchaikovsky's musical abilities were already quite evident by age five, as was his hypersensitivity. His mother died when he was fourteen, a painful event that some say prompted him to compose. Over the years he was plagued by sexual scandals and episodes we might call "nervous breakdowns" today. Historians have uncovered evidence that his death, which was officially listed as having been caused by cholera, was actually a suicide. Many believe that the composer knowingly drank water tainted with cholera. Tchaikovsky's work stands as some of the most essentially Russian music in the classical repertoire, yet he was not a part of the Russian nationalistic school. In fact he was treated quite cruelly by critics of his day. "Tchaikovsky's Piano Concerto No. 1, like the first pancake, is a flop," wrote a St. Petersburg critic in 1875. A Boston critic claimed that his Symphony No. 6 ("Pathétique") "...threads all the foul ditches and sewers of human despair; it is as unclean as music can well be." For all the vehement criticism the composer received during his lifetime, his works are now among the best loved of the classical repertoire. His ballet *The Nutcracker* is an international holiday classic, while *Swan Lake* is a staple in the repertoire of ballet companies throughout the world. His *1812 Overture* is among the most recognizable of all classical pieces. In 1893 the composer completed work on his Symphony No. 6. The first movement dealt with themes of passion, the second with romance, the third with disillusionment and the finale with death. The piece was premiered on October 28. Nine days later the composer was dead.

Lullaby
(Wiegenlied)

Johannes Brahms
1830–1897
Op. 49, No. 4
originally for voice and piano

Symphony No. 1
Fourth Movement Excerpt

Johannes Brahms
1830–1897
Op. 68
originally for orchestra

Allegro non troppo ma con brio

Symphony No. 4

First Movement Excerpt

Johannes Brahms
1830-1897
Op. 98
originally for orchestra

Allegro non troppo

Polovetzian Dance
from the opera PRINCE IGOR
First Theme

Alexander Borodin
1833-1887
originally for orchestra

original key: A Major

Symphony No. 7
Second Movement Excerpt

Anton Bruckner
1824-1896
originally for orchestra

Adagio

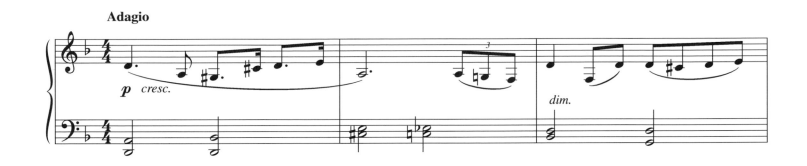

original key: C-sharp minor

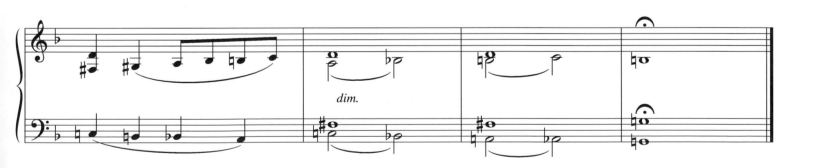

Mazurka in G Minor

Fryderyk Chopin
1810–1849
Op. 67, No. 2 (Posthumous)

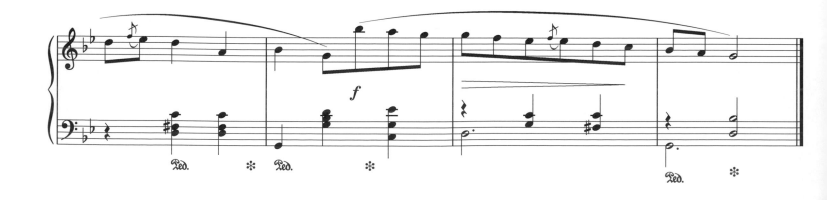

Mazurka in E Minor

Fryderyk Chopin
1810–1849
Op. 17, No. 2

Lento, ma non troppo ♩ = 144

Nocturne in C-sharp Minor

Fryderyk Chopin
1810–1849
Op. Posthumous

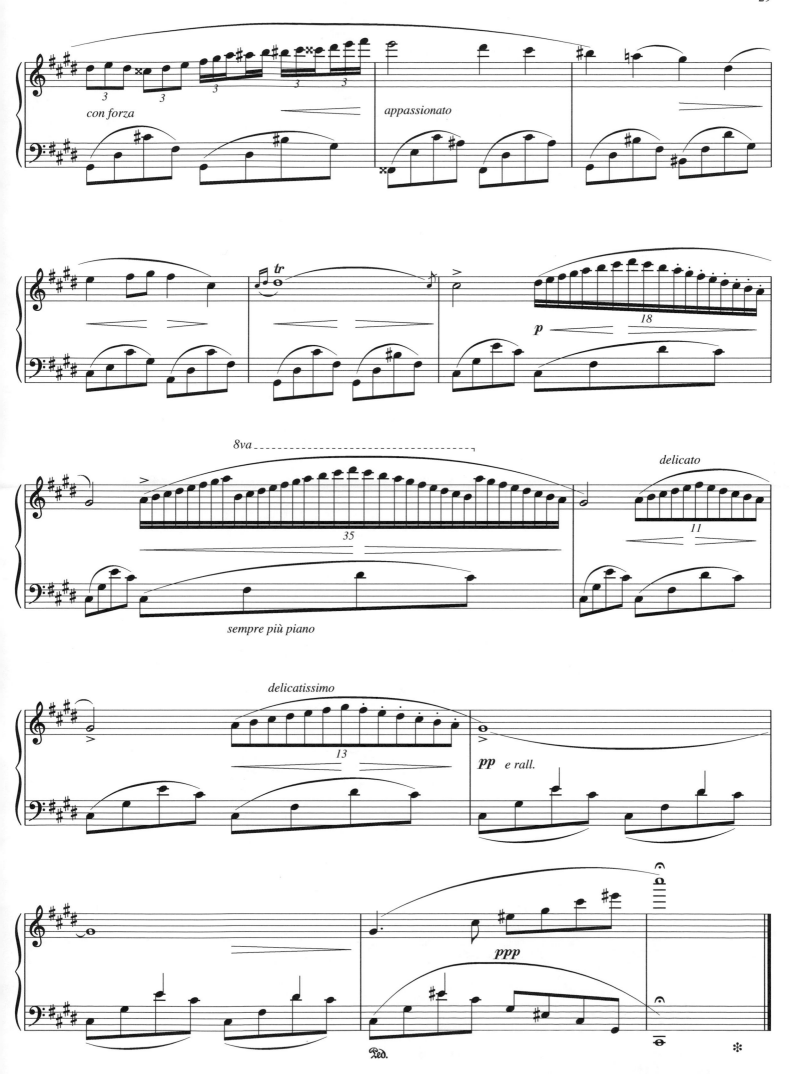

Prelude in A Major

Fryderyk Chopin
1810–1849
Op. 28, No. 7

Mazurka in F Major

Fryderyk Chopin
1810–1849
Op. 68, No. 3 (Posthumous)

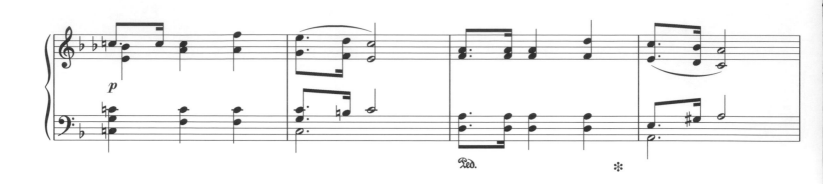

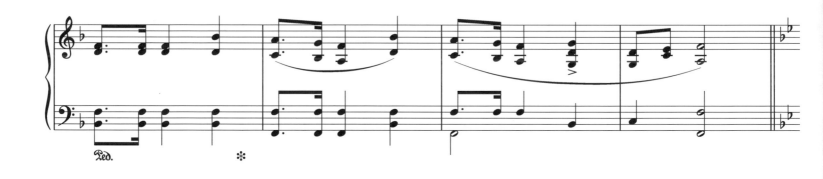

Poco più vivo

Prelude in C Minor

Fryderyk Chopin
1810–1849
Op. 28, No. 20

Polonaise in G Minor

Fryderyk Chopin
1810–1849
Op. Posthumous

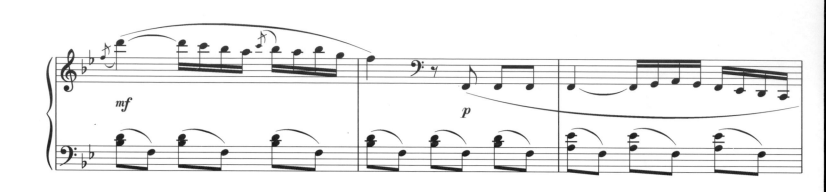

Trio

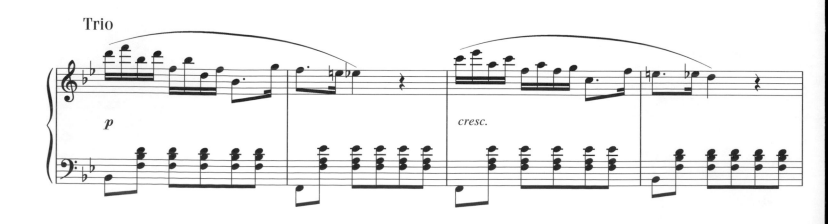

Polonaise da capo al fine

Prelude in B Minor

Fryderyk Chopin
1810-1849
Op. 28, No. 6

Prelude in E Minor

Fryderyk Chopin
1810–1849
Op. 28, No. 4

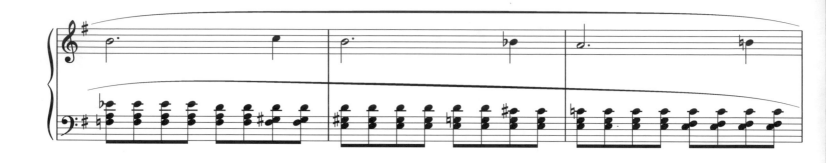

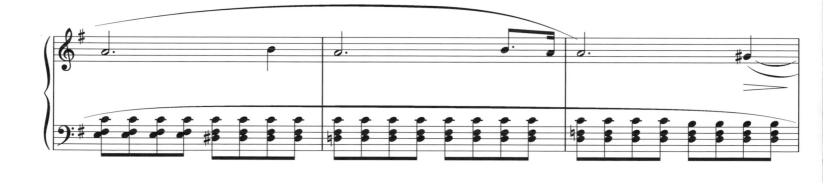

Waltz in B Minor

Fryderyk Chopin
1810–1849
Op. 69, No. 2 (Posthumous)

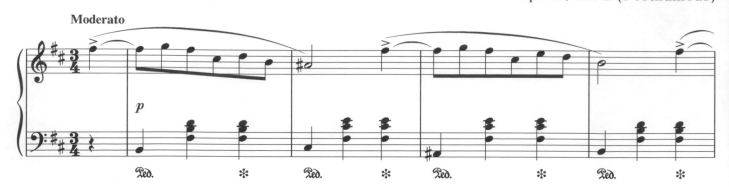

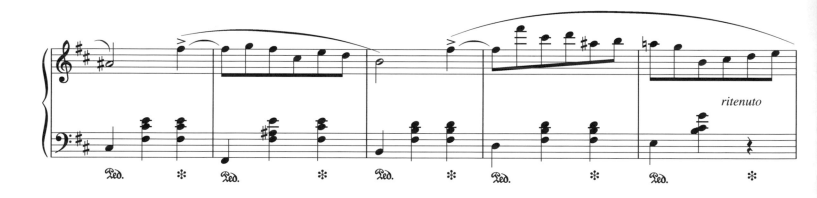

Waltz in F Minor

Fryderyk Chopin
1810–1849
Op. 70, No. 2

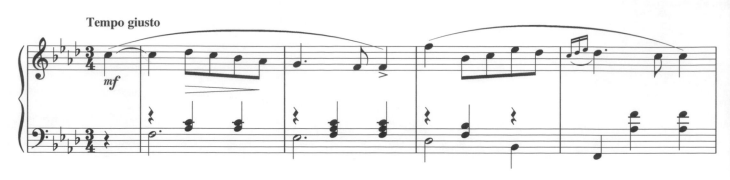

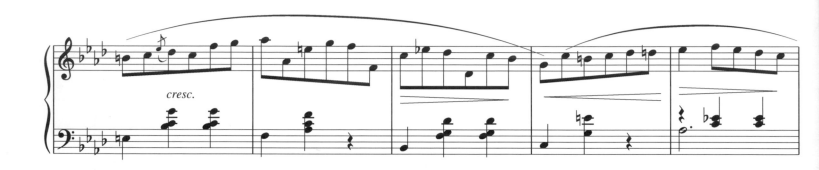

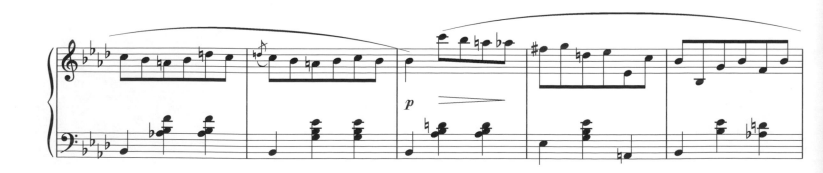

Panis angelicus

César Franck
1822-1890
originally for tenor and
instrumental ensemble

Funeral March of a Marionette

Themes

Charles Gounod
1818-1893
originally for orchestra

Allegretto

Arietta

from LYRIC PIECES, BOOK 1

Edvard Grieg
1843–1907
Op. 12, No. 1

Poco andante e sostenuto

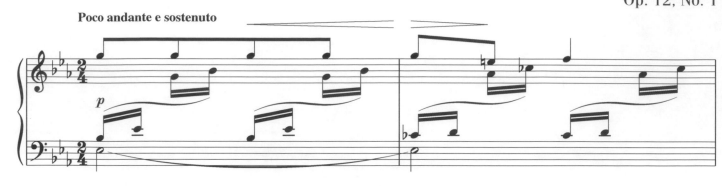

Album Leaf
from LYRIC PIECES, BOOK 1

Edvard Grieg
1843-1907
Op. 12, No. 7

Allegretto e dolce

Elves' Dance
from LYRIC PIECES, BOOK 1

Edvard Grieg
1843-1907
Op. 12, No.4

Molto Allegro e sempre staccato

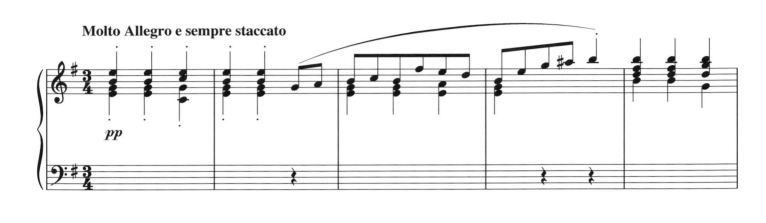

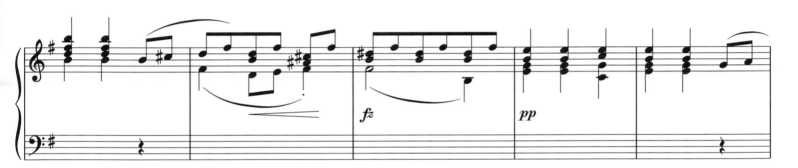

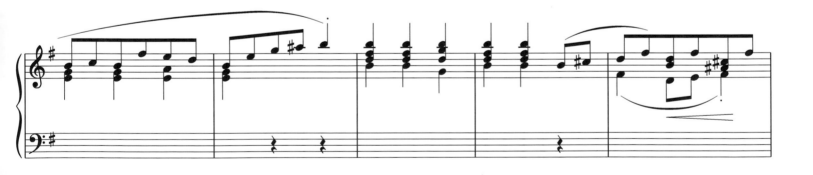

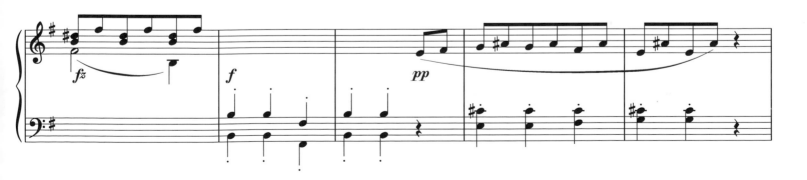

Watchman's Song
from LYRIC PIECES, BOOK 1

Edvard Grieg
1843–1907
Op. 12, No. 3

INTERMEZZO
Spirit of the Night

Waltz
from LYRIC PIECES, BOOK 1

Edvard Grieg
1843-1907
Op. 12, No. 2

Allegro moderato

CODA

Cradle Song
from LYRIC PIECES, BOOK 9

Edvard Grieg
1843-1907
Op. 68, No. 5

Allegretto tranquillamente

Grandmother's Minuet

from LYRIC PIECES, BOOK 9

Edvard Grieg
1843-1907
Op. 68, No. 2

Allegretto grazioso e leggierissimo

Tempo I

In the Hall of the Mountain King

from PEER GYNT

Edvard Grieg
1843-1907
Op. 23, No. 7
originally for orchestra

Alla marcia e molto marcato

78

The Fair
from ALBUM LEAVES FOR THE YOUNG

Cornelius Gurlitt
1820–1901
Op. 101, No. 8

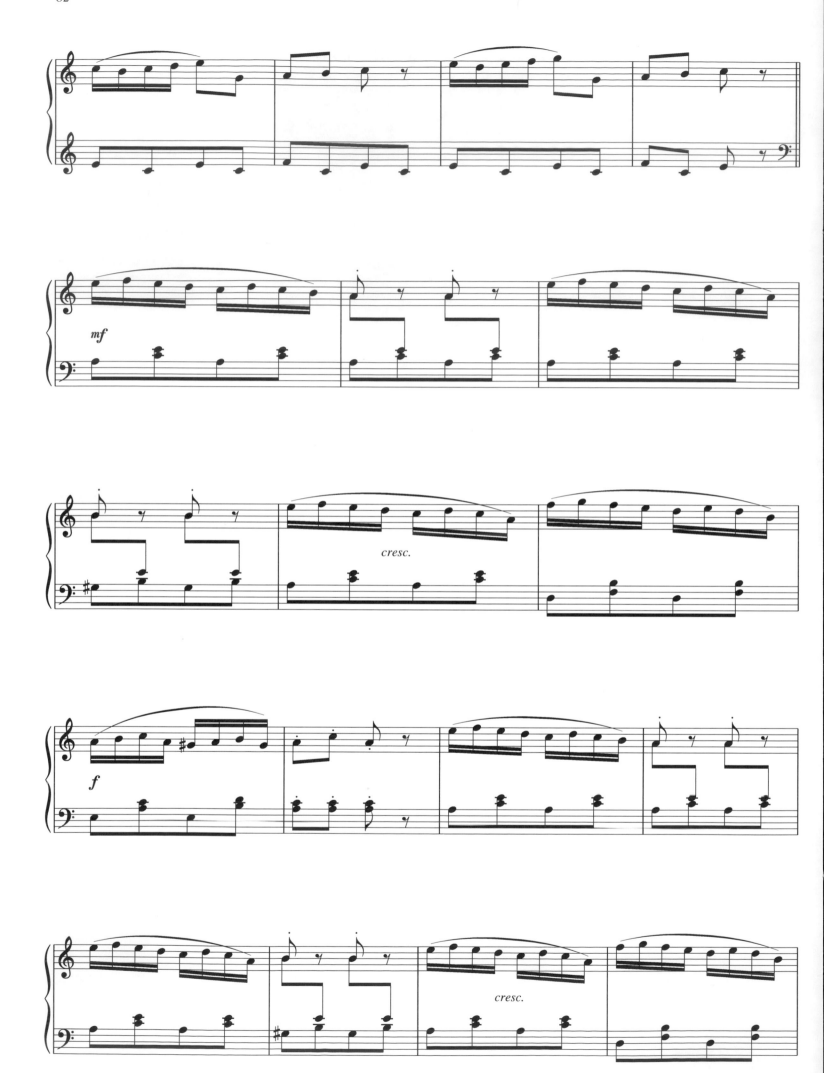

March

from ALBUM LEAVES FOR THE YOUNG

Cornelius Gurlitt
1820–1901
Op. 101, No. 1

Vivace, ma non troppo

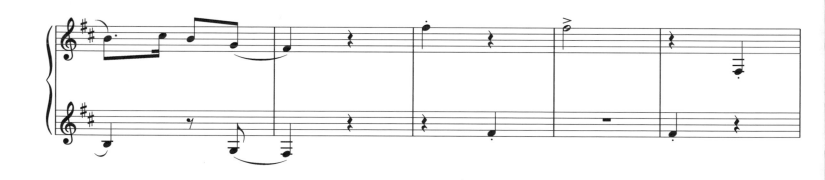

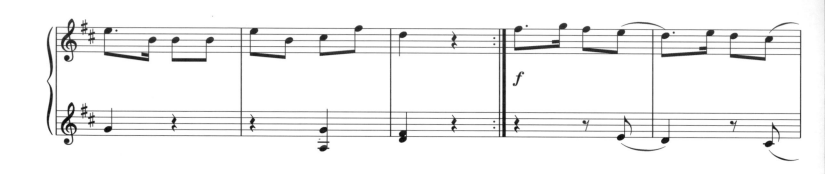

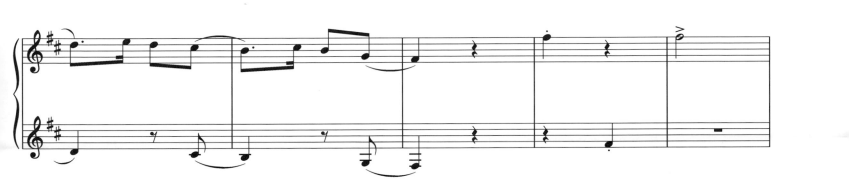

Slumber Song
from ALBUM LEAVES FOR THE YOUNG

Cornelius Gurlitt
1820–1901
Op. 101, No. 6

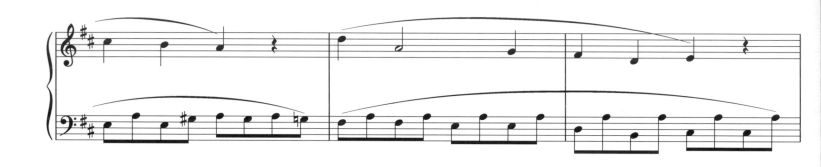

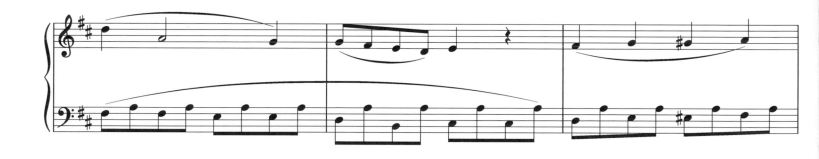

The Brook

Stephen Heller
1813–1888
Op. 45, No. 1

Allegretto

Avalanche

Stephen Heller
1813-1888
Op. 45, No. 2

Allegro vivace

poco meno mosso

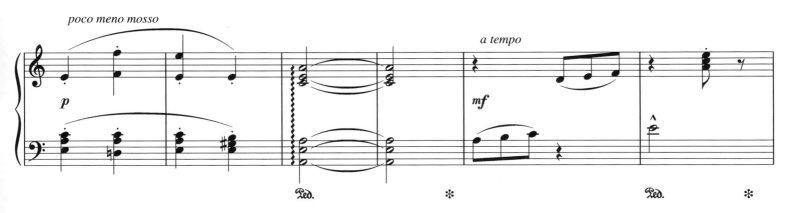

Etude in C Major

Stephen Heller
1813-1888
Op. 47, No. 19

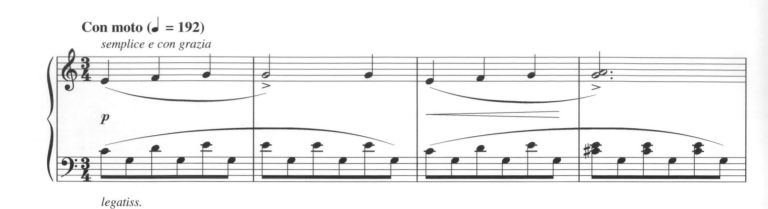

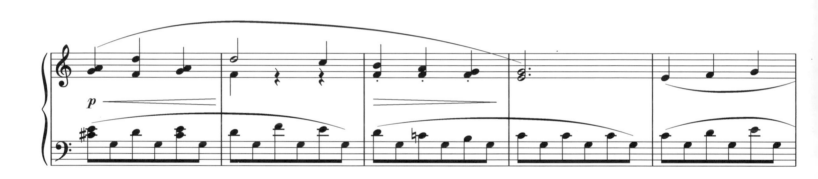

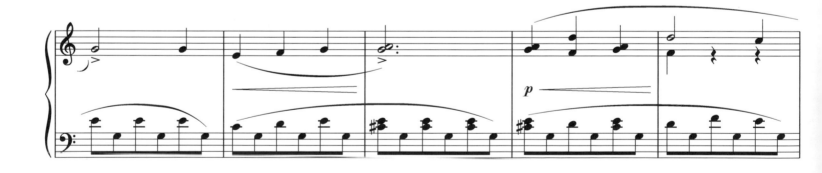

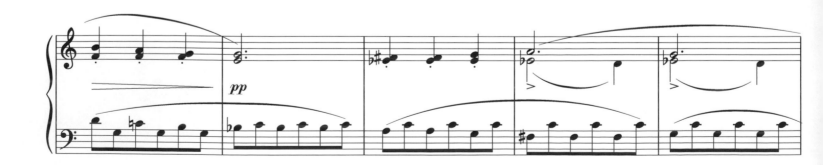

The Tolling Bell

Stephen Heller
1813-1888
Op. 125, No. 8

Prelude in C Minor

Stephen Heller
1813-1888
Op. 119, No. 25

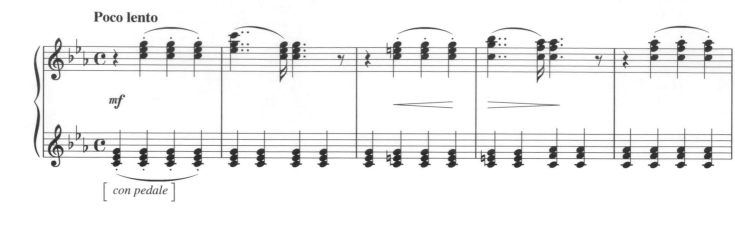

Song of May

Stephen Heller
1813–1888
Op. 45, No. 5

Allegretto comodo

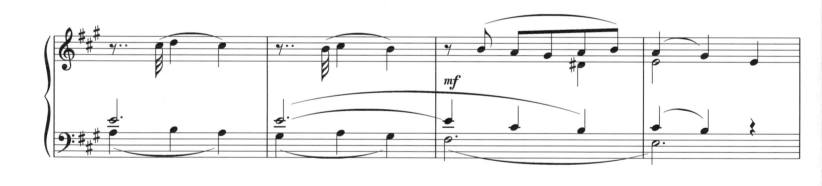

To a Wild Rose
from WOODLAND SKETCHES

Edward MacDowell
1860–1908
Op. 51

Symphony No. 5
Fourth Movement Excerpt ("Adagietto")

Gustav Mahler
1860-1911
this movement originally
for strings and harp

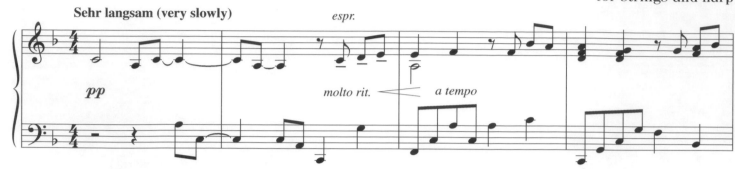

Confidence
from SONGS WITHOUT WORDS

Felix Mendelssohn
1809-1847
Op. 19, No. 4

Regrets
from SONGS WITHOUT WORDS

Felix Mendelssohn
1809–1847
Op. 19, No. 2

Andante espressivo

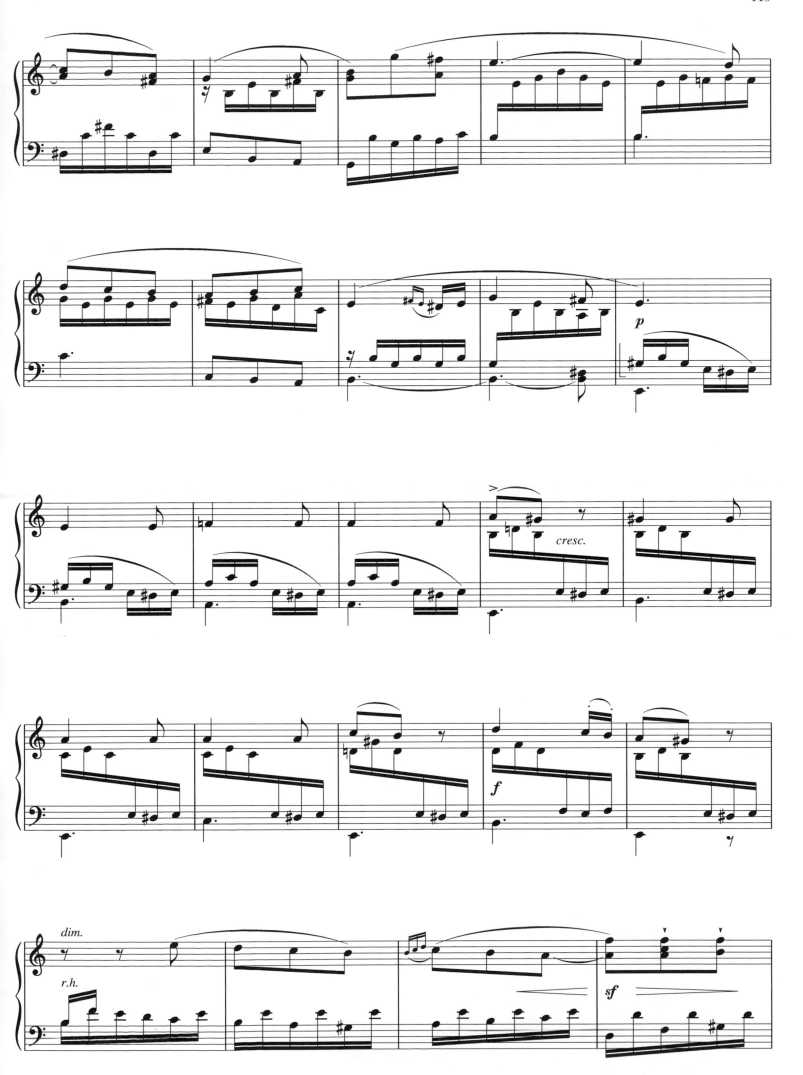

Venetian Boat Song No. 1
from SONGS WITHOUT WORDS

Felix Mendelssohn
1809-1847
Op. 19, No. 6

Andante sostenuto

Consolation
from SONGS WITHOUT WORDS

Felix Mendelssohn
1809–1841
Op. 30, No. 3

Adagio non troppo

Faith
from SONGS WITHOUT WORDS

Felix Mendelssohn
1809-1847
Op. 102, No. 6

Andante

Venetian Boat Song No. 2
from SONGS WITHOUT WORDS

Felix Mendelssohn
1809–1847
Op. 30, No. 6

Tarantella
from SONGS WITHOUT WORDS

Felix Mendelssohn
1809-1847
Op. 102, No. 3

Presto

"Fingal's Cave" Overture

or "The Hebrides"
Themes

Felix Mendelssohn
1809-1847
Op. 26
originally for orchestra

Allegro moderato

Gondola Song in A Major

Felix Mendelssohn
1809–1847
Composed 1837

Symphony No. 4

"Italian"
First Movement Excerpt

Felix Mendelssohn
1809-1847
Op. 90
originally for orchestra

original key: A Major

Meditation
from the opera THAÏS

Jules Massenet
1842-1912

138

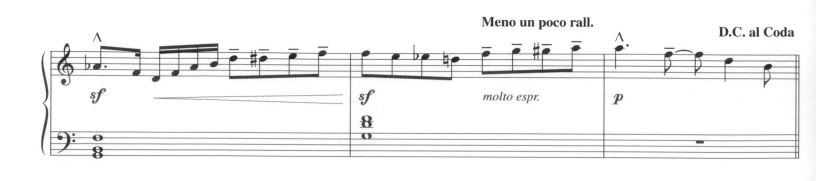

CODA

A Tempo

Calmato

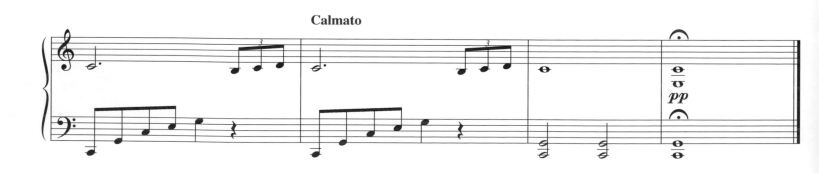

Piano Concerto No. 2
First Movement Excerpt

Sergei Rachmaninoff
1873-1943
Op. 18
originally for piano and orchestra

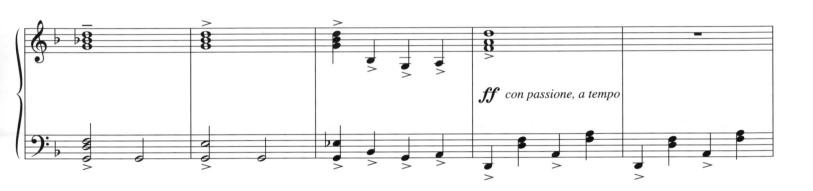

original key: C Minor

Sheherazade

Themes from Part 1

Nikolay Andreyevich Rimsky-Korsakov
1844-1908
Op. 35
originally for orchestra

Allegro non troppo

148

Ecossaise in D Major

(German Dance)

Franz Schubert
1797-1828
Op. 33, No. 2

Andante in C Major

Franz Schubert
1797–1828
Composed 1812

Symphony No. 9

"The Great"
First Movement Excerpt

Franz Schubert
1797-1828
D. 944
published posthumously
originally for orchestra

Andante

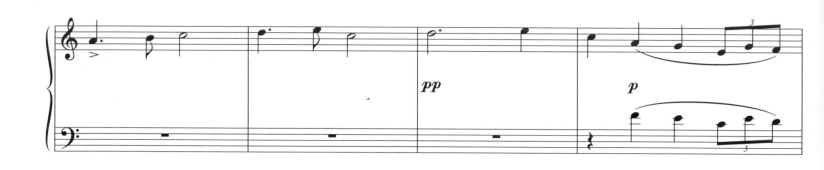

Moment Musicale

Franz Schubert
1797-1828
Op. 94, No. 3

Waltz in A-flat Major

Franz Schubert
1797-1828
Op. 9, No. 12

Waltz in A Major

Franz Schubert
1797–1828
Op. 50, No. 13

Waltz in A Minor

Franz Schubert
1797–1828
D. 969 (Op. 77, No. 9)

Waltz in A-flat Major

Franz Schubert
1797–1828
Op. 33, No. 15

Waltz in F Minor

Franz Schubert
1797–1828
Op. 33, No. 14

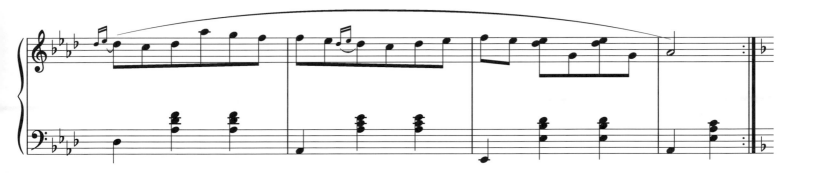

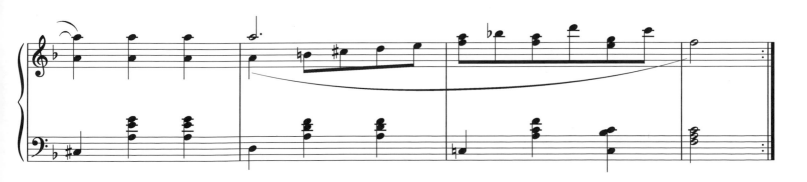

Waltz in B Minor

Franz Schubert
1797–1828
D. 145 (Op. 18a, No. 5)

[Allegro moderato]

pp

cresc.

Waltz in G Major

Franz Schubert
1797-1828
Op. 67, No. 15

Of Strange Lands and People

(Von fremden Ländern und Menschen)
from KINDERSZENEN
(Scenes from Childhood)

Robert Schumann
1810-1856
Op. 15, No. 1

A Child Falling Asleep

(Kind im Einschlummern)
from KINDERSZENEN
(Scenes from Childhood)

Robert Schumann
1810-1856
Op. 15, No. 12

Curious Story
(Curiose Geschichte)
from KINDERSZENEN
(Scenes from Childhood)

Robert Schumann
1810-1856
Op. 15, No. 2

Frightening

(Fürchtenmachen)
from KINDERSZENEN
(Scenes from Childhood)

Robert Schumann
1810-1856
Op. 15, No. 11

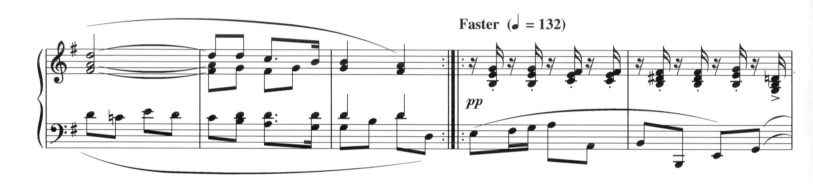

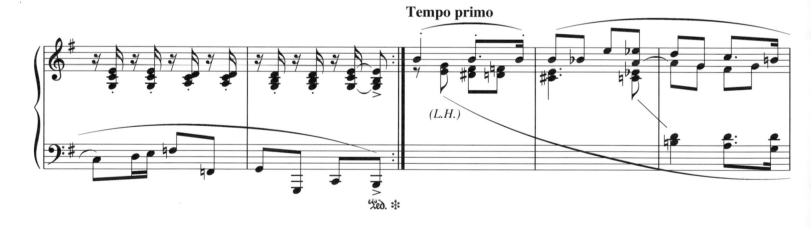

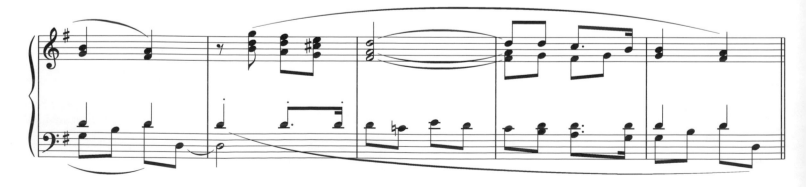

An Important Event

(Wichtige Begebenheit)
from KINDERSZENEN
(Scenes from Childhood)

Robert Schumann
1810-1856
Op. 15, No. 6

The Poet Speaks

(Der Dichter spricht)
from KINDERSZENEN
(Scenes from Childhood)

Robert Schumann
1810-1856
Op. 15, No. 13

Pleading Child

(Bittendes Kind)
from KINDERSZENEN
(Scenes from Childhood)

Robert Schumann
1810-1856
Op. 15, No. 4

Perfectly Contented

(Glückes genug)

from KINDERSZENEN

(Scenes from Childhood)

Robert Schumann
1810-1856
Op. 15, No. 5

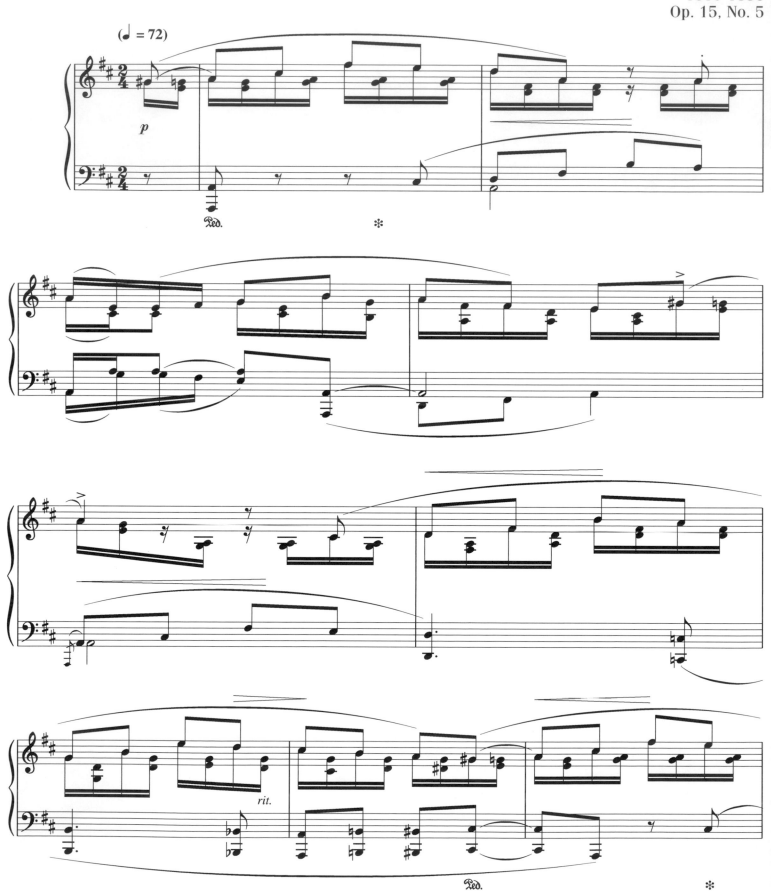

Träumerei
(Reverie)
from KINDERSZENEN
(Scenes from Childhood)

Robert Schumann
1810-1856
Op. 15, No. 7

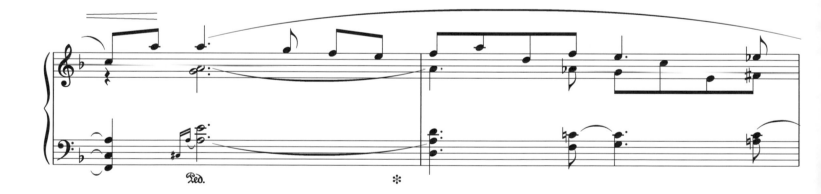

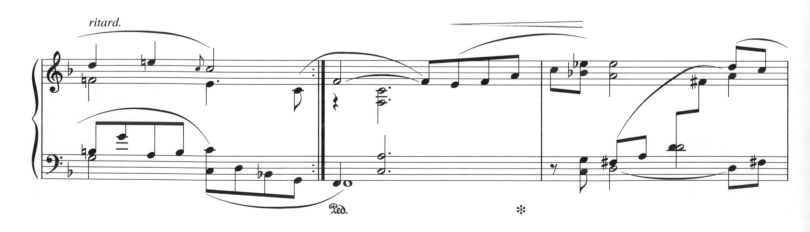

First Loss

from ALBUM FÜR DIE JUGEND

(Album for the Young)

Robert Schumann
1810-1856
Op. 68, No. 16

Moderato ♩ = 88

The Happy Farmer Returning from Work

(Frölicher Landmann, von der Arbeit zurückkehrend)
from ALBUM FÜR DIE JUGEND
(Album for the Young)

Robert Schumann
1810-1856
Op. 68, No. 10

Hunting Song

(Jägerliedchen)
from ALBUM FÜR DIE JUGEND
(Album for the Young)

Robert Schumann
1810-1856
Op. 68, No. 7

Vivace ♩. = 100

Melody
from ALBUM FÜR DIE JUGEND
(Album for the Young)

Robert Schumann
1810-1856
Op. 68, No. 1

The Reaper's Song

(Schnitterliedchen)
from ALBUM FÜR DIE JUGEND
(Album for the Young)

Robert Schumann
1810-1856
Op. 68, No. 18

Allegro moderato ♩. = 108

Soldier's March

(Soldatenmarsch)
from ALBUM FÜR DIE JUGEND
(Album for the Young)

Robert Schumann
1810-1856
Op. 68, No. 2

The Wild Horseman

(Wilder Reiter)

from ALBUM FÜR DIE JUGEND

(Album for the Young)

Robert Schumann
1810-1856
Op. 68, No. 8

Allegro con brio ♩. = 116

Bagatelle

Robert Schumann
1810–1856

Cradle Song

(Wiegenliedchen)
from ALBUMBLÄTTER
(Album Leaves)

Robert Schumann
1810-1856
Op. 124, No. 6

Evensong
from SONATA IN D MAJOR

Robert Schumann
1810–1856
Op. 118b

Fantasy Dance

Robert Schumann
1810–1856
Op. 124, No. 5

Waltz

Robert Schumann
1810–1856
Op. 129, No. 4

Tales from the Vienna Woods

Themes

Johann Strauss, Jr.
1825-1899
Op. 325
originally for orchestra

By the Beautiful Blue Danube

Themes

Johann Strauss, Jr.
1825-1899
Op. 317
originally for orchestra

1812 Overture

Excerpt

Pyotr Il'yich Tchaikovsky
1840-1893
Op. 49
originally for orchestra

Dance of the Sugar Plum Fairy

from the ballet THE NUTCRACKER

Pyotr Il'yich Tchaikovsky
1840-1893
Op. 71
originally for orchestra

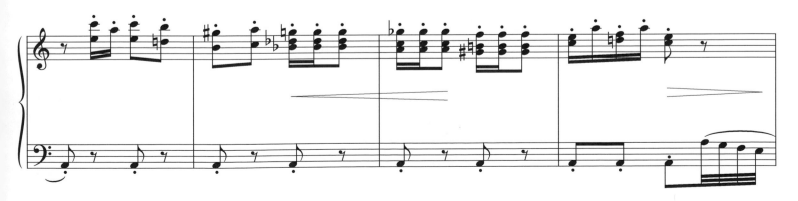

original key: E Minor

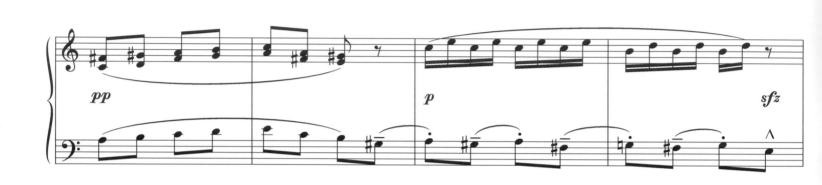

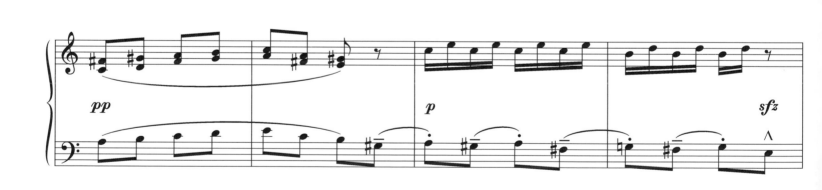

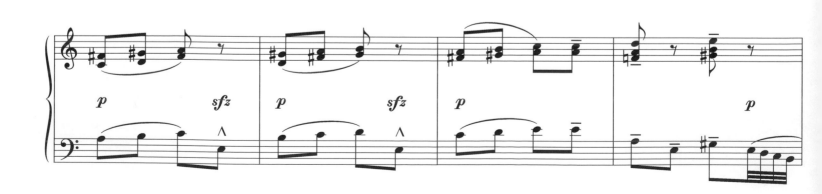

In Church

from ALBUM FOR CHILDREN
(Album pour enfants)

Pyotr Il'yich Tchaikovsky
1840-1893
Op. 39, No. 24

Andantino (♩ = 58)

The Hobby Horse

from ALBUM FOR CHILDREN
(Album pour enfants)

Pyotr Il'yich Tchaikovsky
1840-1893
Op. 39, No. 3

Morning Prayer
from ALBUM FOR CHILDREN
(Album pour enfants)

Pyotr Il'yich Tchaikovsky
1840–1893
Op. 39, No. 1

Italian Song

from ALBUM FOR CHILDREN
(Album pour enfants)

Pyotr Il'yich Tchaikovsky
1840-1893
Op. 39, No. 15

Mazurka

from ALBUM FOR CHILDREN
(Album pour enfants)

Pyotr Il'yich Tchaikovsky
1840–1893
Op. 39, No. 10

Tempo di Mazurka

Old French Song

from ALBUM FOR CHILDREN
(Album pour enfants)

Pyotr Il'yich Tchaikovsky
1840-1893
Op. 39, No. 16

The Organ Grinder

from ALBUM FOR CHILDREN
(Album pour enfants)

Pyotr Il'yich Tchaikovsky
1840-1893
Op. 39, No. 23

Polka

from ALBUM FOR CHILDREN
(Album pour enfants)

Pyotr Il'yich Tchaikovsky
1840-1893
Op. 39, No. 14

Russian Song

from ALBUM FOR CHILDREN
(Album pour enfants)

Pyotr Il'yich Tchaikovsky
1840-1893
Op. 39, No. 11

The Sick Doll

from ALBUM FOR CHILDREN
(Album pour enfants)

Pyotr Il'yich Tchaikovsky
1840-1893
Op. 39, No. 6

The Song of the Lark

from ALBUM FOR CHILDREN
(Album pour enfants)

Pyotr Il'yich Tchaikovsky
1840-1893
Op. 39, No. 22

Sweet Dream

from ALBUM FOR CHILDREN
(Album pour enfants)

Pyotr Il'yich Tchaikovsky
1840-1893
Op. 39, No. 21

Waltz in E-flat Major

from ALBUM FOR CHILDREN
(Album pour enfants)

Pyotr Il'yich Tchaikovsky
1840–1893
Op. 39, No. 8

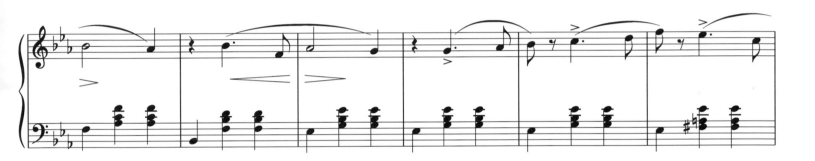

Piano Concerto No. 1
First Movement Excerpt

Pyotr Il'yich Tchaikovsky
1840-1893
Op. 23
originally for piano and orchestra

Andante maestoso

original key: B-flat Minor

ROMEO AND JULIET

Fantasy Overture
"Love Theme"

Pyotr Il'yich Tchaikovsky
1840-1893
originally for orchestra

Allegro giusto, con espressione

original key: D-flat Major

Waltz of the Flowers

from the ballet THE NUTCRACKER
Excerpt

Pyotr Il'yich Tchaikovsky
1840-1893
Op. 71
originally for orchestra

original key: D Major